NINE TO FIVE

ON THE SIDE:

A PROVEN PATH TO ENTREPRENEURIAL SUCCESS

TaKenya J. White, ATR

NINE TO FIVE ON THE SIDE: A PROVEN PATH TO
ENTREPRENEURIAL SUCCESS
Copyright © 2025 by TAKENYA WHITE

All rights reserved. No part of this book may be reproduced or transmitted in any form or by any means without written permission from the author.

Printed in the USA

CREDITS

This work was not created in isolation. It reflects the encouragement, expertise, and steady presence of those who supported the process in seen and unseen ways.

Foreword
Ambrose Panico

Editorial Support
Kat Simond Communications

Professional Contribution
Aleicha Addison, CPA

Creative & Strategic Development
TaKenya Jene'a White, ATR

Design & Production
Expressive Arts Services LLC

Community & Encouragement
To the educators, creatives, entrepreneurs, clients, and students

whose lived experiences informed the reflection, questions, and insight within these pages.

Acknowledgments

I want to first thank my family, my mom and my brothers, for being my constant support throughout every season of life. You have been my greatest sounding boards, always offering love, honesty, and respect. Your words, whether spoken in laughter or truth, have grounded me in every phase of becoming. I am deeply grateful for your presence and your unwavering belief in me.

To my nephew, my first Boo, my child before I ever had a child, and to my daughter, my Maree-Boo, my heart and motivation, thank you both for being my inspiration. You've given me the courage to keep building, even when the days were long and the vision felt far away. You've worked beside me, cheered for me, and believed in me when I needed it most. Everything I create is with you in mind and for the legacy we are building together.

To my close friends, those who never wavered and continued to have faith in my assignment, thank you. You have seen the vision from the beginning and encouraged me toward it with prayer, patience, and accountability. Your faith in me helped me keep faith in myself.

Lastly, I want to thank my spiritual advisors, who have poured into me for more than twenty years. The wisdom of your voices echoes in my spirit as I write these words. Your guidance has shaped my understanding of purpose, leadership, and divine timing. I am grateful for your covering, your counsel, and your constant reminders to "stay in faith."

Thank you, all of you, for being a part of my journey. This work is a reflection of the love, faith, and community that surrounds me.

TABLE OF CONTENTS

Table Of Contents	**6**
Foreword	**8**
Preface	**12**
Chapter One	**16**
Do It for You, Write the Vision	16
Chapter Two	**25**
Identifying Your Gifts, Talents & Areas You Are Naturally Adept	25
Chapter Three	**32**
Living in This World, Not of This World	32
Chapter Four	**38**
Protecting Your Vision	38
Chapter Five	**47**
Mastery In Motion	47
Chapter Six	**59**
Delayed Gratification	59
Chapter Seven	**65**
Purposeful Connections	65
Chapter Eight	**73**
Personal Finances	73
Financial Foundations	87
from a CPA's Perspective	87
Chapter Nine	**90**
You Are a Service Provider	90

Chapter Ten	**96**
Partnerships	**96**
Chapter Eleven	**106**
Legacy and Leadership	**106**
Chapter Twelve	**112**
When Purpose Becomes Primary	**112**
Scriptural Appendix & Index	**119**

Foreword

There are *how-to* books, and then there are *seminal* books. **Nine To Five On The Side** belongs to the latter. It emerged from a life well-considered.

When TaKenya asked me to write the foreword for her book, I was honored, happy for her, and excited to see what she had created, but certainly not surprised. I knew this book was inside her, perhaps even before she knew it herself. "T," as I affectionately refer to her, is a gentle force, but a force, nonetheless.

We worked together at a public elementary school serving emotionally challenged children. She was an Art Therapist, and I was a consultant charged with building classroom communities. If you read this book, you will learn that "T" believes it was Divine Intervention that brought us together. While the circumstances may have appeared practical, I have learned that meaningful connections often arrive through ordinary moments. Either way, I consider our shared classroom a gift.

Sharing a classroom meant that two people who could have remained polite, "Good morning, how are you?" Professional acquaintances instead became colleagues, confidants, partners, and good friends.

It was between the covers of **Nine To Five On The Side** that I realized that while I was simply moving through my days, my friend was quietly *Protecting Her Vision* (Chapter 4). She was being i*ntentionally selective*. "T" had decided that sharing a classroom was not just an assignment, but an opportunity she chose to embrace through *Mastery in Motion* (Chapter 5).

That classroom became a space where two like-minded people exchanged insights and offered one another counsel, not only about our nine-to-five responsibilities and our students, but also about ourselves and our goals beyond the workday.

In Chapter 7, *Purposeful Connections*, "T" writes:

"You don't need to be in every room. You need to be in the right ones. You need people, spaces, and opportunities that reflect where you are going, not just where you have been."

I am one of "T's" people, and she is one of mine.

That belief in purposeful connection eventually led me to work with TaKenya and The Content House to grow my professional development and motivational speaking company. **Nine To Five On The Side** is a proven path, but it is more than a business guide. It is wisdom shaped by experience, reflection, and intentional growth.

This book challenges you. It encourages you to discern real opportunities from distractions. And most importantly, it builds the confidence required to walk your own path.

Do the work. Keep the faith.

Ambrose Panico
Owner & President, Behave Yourself LLP

Preface

This book was written for those who feel the quiet pull towards purpose; a sense that there is something more to build, more to become, and more to give. It's for the dreamers who have spent years working for others, yet feel a growing desire to create something of their own. It's for the builders, the believers, and the ones who know deep down that the work of their hands holds a deeper meaning. The lessons, challenges, and revelations shared here come from my own entrepreneurial journey. I didn't begin with a blueprint or a clear map; I learned through trial, reflection, and faith. Each step revealed something new about resilience and purpose; lessons I now offer to help others move forward with greater confidence, and flow.

Nine to Five On the Side is not just about entrepreneurship; it's about stepping into purpose. It's about discovering your gifts, trusting your timing, and learning to move with divine flow rather than force. It invites you to look at your current environment, not as a limitation, but as a training ground. Each chapter is designed to guide you from intention to implementation and ultimately from working for someone else's vision to fully walking in your own.

Throughout these pages, you'll find reflections drawn from my personal experiences, as an entrepreneur, a therapist, and a believer, alongside spiritual truths that have shaped my journey. You'll also encounter biblical references and principles that offer wisdom, motivation, and grounding. While the roots of this book are deeply connected to my faith, its message speaks to universal human experiences: growth, faith, resilience, and purpose.

You do not need to share my beliefs to find connection here. Purpose transcends labels and beliefs. It is a divine thread that runs through every life, calling each of us to *be,* create, serve, and lead in our own unique way.

As you read, take your time. Reflect. Write in the margins. Revisit the exercises and journaling prompts. Allow the words to meet you where you are and give yourself permission to grow without pressure or perfection. Purpose doesn't rush; it unfolds.

May this book remind you that your purpose is not waiting for you to quit your job, earn a title, or receive validation. It's already alive within you. My hope is that these words help you nurture it, protect it, and prepare it to flourish, both in business and in life.

Move in faith. Build with intention. Flow.

— *TaKenya Jene'a*

NINE TO FIVE ON THE SIDE: A PROVEN PATH TO ENTREPRENEURIAL SUCCESS

CHAPTER 1

Chapter One

Do It for You, Write the Vision

The Importance of Why and What?

Imagine waking to soft morning light and the faint whisper of wind. Your body moves slowly, guided by intention rather than urgency. You breathe in gratitude before your feet even touch the floor.

You take a moment to settle your spirit. You may meditate, pray, or simply sit in quiet stillness and allow yourself to ease into the day.

You reach for your morning drink, feeling the warmth or coolness of the cup as you look out the window. You watch your neighborhood come alive. Cars move gently down the street. Children chatter as they head toward school. The world begins its familiar rhythm, and you smile with appreciation. You are grateful for the pause, for the stillness, for the freedom to move at your own pace.

This is the life you designed, a life that allows you to breathe, create, and lead without rushing to satisfy the imposed expectations of traditional employment.

This does not mean the absence of responsibility. It means your work no longer controls your time in ways that conflict with how you are called to live.

I once imagined mornings like this long before I knew they were possible.

Now take a moment to imagine your own perfect beginning. If you could design the first hour of your day to support the life you deeply desire, what would it include? What would you see, hear, or feel? Would your morning carry stillness or movement, silence or song?

Whatever it looks like, remember this truth: it is not fantasy. It is an invitation to glimpse what becomes possible when your work fully supports your life. Consider it a subtle preview; a vision that helps guide your work, your business, and the decisions that shape the life you want to build, not a demand that you arrive there now.

I am not promising every day will feel calm. Life, family, and business will bring busy moments. But you hold the authority to determine how full your days become. You choose when your day begins, when you work, and how you spend your energy. You can design your business and your life in a rhythm that supports you.

This is the first gift of choosing to do it for you.

Choosing to do it for you does not mean changing everything at once. It means allowing your vision to lead before your circumstances fully catch up.

Clarity and Lifestyle Alignment

Before stepping fully into entrepreneurship, you need a clear picture of what fits your life right now. Consider the responsibilities you have chosen, whether family, work, community, or caregiving. These are not burdens. They represent what you have committed to love.

When shaping a business or side venture, build around the life you actually have, not the one you imagine you are supposed to have. When your work resonates with your real life, it becomes something you can sustain with joy instead of pressure.

Clarity of vision rarely arrives all at once. It grows through honest self-reflection. Ask yourself: What do I want my days to look like? Who do I feel called to serve? What would peace look like in this season?

These questions form the blueprint that guides your next steps.

Divine Design and Uniqueness

If you believe in divine design as I do, then you already understand this truth: you were created with intention. You were never meant to be a copy, a repeat, or a muted version of someone else's story. Your thoughts, your perspective, and the way your mind organizes ideas are distinctly your own.

Think about trees. Even when planted at the same time, in the same soil, under the same sky, no two grow exactly in the same way. Science confirms what nature quietly demonstrates every day: each tree develops its own structure, contributes differently to the ecosystem, and plays a role that no other tree can fully replace. Their uniqueness is not accidental; it is essential to the health of the whole (Alimpić et al., 2022).

When trees line a landscape, their beauty does not come from sameness, but from variation. Each one strengthens the environment through its individual presence. They may be similar in composition, but each carries its own shape, texture, and history. The same is true for us.

Some of your ideas may feel familiar. That does not diminish their value. Just as forests rely on diversity to remain resilient, your perspective matters because it is shaped by your personal history, your passion, and your insight. What you contribute cannot be substituted.

That blend creates your divine signature.

When you quiet your voice or withhold your gifts, the world misses something it cannot receive from anyone else. Your creativity, your methods, and your rhythm all reveal a part of creation only you can carry.

The Power of Releasing What Is Within

There is a deep and steady satisfaction that comes from releasing what has been living inside you, not for praise, but simply because it belongs in the world.

Doing it for you means you create, build, or express because it fulfills something internal. You are not waiting for approval. You are honoring the purpose within you.

When you release your ideas, you awaken confidence and strengthen your faith. You prove to yourself that you can bring vision into form.

It is never about perfection. It is about responding to what stirs your spirit. That stirring may arrive quietly, as a recurring thought, a gentle awareness, or a steady pull that invites your attention. Each time you honor that inner nudge, you strengthen the relationship between your spirit and your discipline.

With repetition, this response becomes familiar. Your spirit recognizes that it is acknowledged, and your discipline learns how to support what matters in you the most. You begin to move with intention, guided by attentiveness and care. There is a rhythm that forms, one shaped by consistency.

This is where purpose becomes practice. Purpose takes shape through your daily responses and the choices you make when you listen inwardly. It is expressed through steady action, presence, and follow-through. In this way, purpose is lived, not pursued, and practice becomes a natural extension of what already resonates within you.

Writing the Vision

Writing is documentation and direction. When you place your vision on paper, you move it from thought into form, from unseen to visible. You create something you can return to, refine, and eventually act upon.

Documenting vision extends beyond simply writing. It can be marked through creative expression, through daily choices, and through speaking it aloud, giving vision a place to live. It keeps your direction clear and your intention present as you move forward.

Begin with something simple. Write what you want your life to reflect, not only the goals you hope to reach, but the way you want to feel while reaching them. Let your words come from faith rather than fear. Writing is a declaration that you are willing to give your vision a place to grow.

Every time you revisit your vision, clarity strengthens. Each word becomes a step toward bringing that vision to life. A written vision becomes your guide when life feels loud or scattered. It reminds you of your direction and your why.

"Write the vision and make it plain."

The Parable of the Talents

There is a story in the Bible about talents, gifts entrusted to different people. Some used what they received and multiplied it.

One person buried theirs out of fear. This is what happens when we withhold what has been placed within us.

Fear, comparison, and uncertainty can convince us to hide our gifts. Yet when you use even one of your abilities, when you release one idea or take one small step, you create room for more. Every act of courage expands your capacity to receive and produce.

Whether you see yourself as multi-talented or not, the responsibility remains the same. Use what has been given to you, the gifts already living within. When you choose to do it for you, you are honoring purpose.

Closing Thought

Doing it for you means taking ownership of your time, your energy, and your gifts. It means writing a vision that rises from truth rather than fear, expectation, or trends.

You are the author of your days. You are the designer of your dreams. As you shape your life and your work, you make room for what already lives within you. Inside each of us are seeds, gifts, and abilities with the potential to create something meaningful.

Clear understanding is the soil that nurtures every intention, and your vision is the seed. In the next chapter, we will explore what has already been planted within you, the gifts and natural strengths that form the raw materials of the life and business you are building.

Chapter 2

Chapter Two

Identifying Your Gifts, Talents & Areas You Are Naturally Adept

Discover what you already carry

Before you can build a business or pursue a dream, you must understand what you are working with. Your gifts and talents are the raw materials of your purpose. Everything you need is already within you. This chapter helps you uncover it.

What Is a Gift?

Oftentimes, when we think of the word "gift," we tend to imagine undeniable abilities that the world celebrates, perhaps the kind that draws a crowd and earns applause.

We think of a vocalist whose tone sends chills through the body, a speaker who can captivate a room, or an Emmy-winning actor like Denzel Washington, who brings truth and depth to every character he inhabits. A painter like Pablo Picasso, who reshaped how we see form and color. Or a composer like Mozart, whose work still echoes through time.

These visible expressions of giftedness are extraordinary, yes, but most gifts begin quietly. They are subtle and steady, yet powerful and transformative.

Let me explain. A gift is the deep, unseen thing that fuels visible expression.
Painting is not what made Picasso gifted; his true gift was perception.

He saw the world in shapes, layers, and hidden dimensions. The canvas was only the vehicle.

Mozart's true gift was not composition alone, but his ability to feel rhythm and emotion so precisely that sound became the language of his inner world.

Denzel Washington doesn't just act. He embodies. His gifts are empathy, discipline, and the ability to translate truth into presence.

When you understand gifts this way, you see that the finished product (the film, the painting, the symphony) is simply evidence. The gift lives deeper.

Put plainly: a gift is what flows through you with ease. It feels natural, intuitive, and energizing. It is often the thing others recognize before you do.

Psychologist Mihaly Csikszentmihalyi describes this experience as *flow*, a state of deep absorption in which a person feels fully present, focused, and internally motivated (Csikszentmihalyi, 1996). Flow often occurs when an individual is engaged in activities that resonate with their natural strengths, where effort feels meaningful rather than draining. These moments of deep engagement can quietly reveal where a person's gifts and natural aptitude reside.

Some gifts speak loudly. Some speak softly. All carry value and purpose.

You may have a gift for relaying messages, organizing chaos, sensing emotional shifts, storytelling, connecting ideas, bringing people comfort, or solving what others avoid. These are not small things. They are tools for building.

Recognizing What Comes Naturally

Before you can expand your gifts, you must notice them.

We overlook what comes easily because ease rarely announces itself. It doesn't feel forced or rehearsed. It simply flows.

Picasso didn't stop mid-stroke to ask, "Am I gifted?"
Mozart didn't question whether he should feel rhythm that deeply.
They followed what was already moving within them.

This is what it looks like when your doing and your being work in harmony.

I'll use myself as an example.

Like Picasso, I paint. But my gift is not the paint itself. My gift is in the way I organize layers of meaning before the brush ever touches the canvas. I am reading tone, emotion, movement, and narrative. I see the image before it exists. That inner blueprint is the gift; the painting is simply the expression.

We often expect gifts to require struggle. But your greatest value often lives in what flows effortlessly.

That ease is not laziness. It is intelligence.

> *"We have different gifts, according to the grace given to each of us."*

Maybe you sense people's needs before they speak. Maybe you see patterns others overlook. Maybe you resolve tension with calmness. Maybe you create order from scattered ideas.

These are quiet forms of genius.

Your gifts often reveal themselves through joy, curiosity, or the feeling of "rightness" you get while doing something that feels harmonious in your soul.

You may be able to build something from someone else's model, but eventually you must insert your own raw materials. Your way of seeing, feeling, and creating is what makes your work uniquely yours.

The Power of Self-Awareness

Knowing your gifts is not only a confidence boost. It is a powerful strategy.

Self-awareness connects who you are, what you do, and why it matters. Without it, you can chase goals that look good but do not feel right. Think of self-awareness as both mirror and compass. The mirror helps you see your strengths, your patterns, and your blind spots. The compass helps you navigate back to what feels true when life or expectation pulls you away.

As I learned to navigate as an artist and entrepreneur, I realized my creativity wasn't confined to my art. It shaped how I build systems, communicate, and help others discover their path. That realization allowed me to stop copying traditional models and instead pave a road that felt natural to me.

This part is hard for many of us because we are constantly shown what success "should" look like. It's easy to blur your identity with someone else's. Self-awareness frees you from imitation.
It makes space for your authentic voice.

Once I honored what worked for me, I found peace and flow.

Closing Thought

Entrepreneurship, like art, is an expression of self. The clearer you are about your gifts, the more intentional your building becomes.

When you create from your strengths, you move differently. You communicate with ease as you recognize opportunities that resonate with your soul. You release what does not align with purpose, and you protect your energy while operating harmoniously.

You do not have to master everything. But you do need to know yourself. Your gifts are not accidental. They are the foundation of what you are called to build.

CHAPTER 3

CHAPTER THREE

LIVING IN THIS WORLD, NOT OF THIS WORLD

You report to an office, but you belong to a Kingdom.

There is a unique tension that comes with being in the world and drawn toward something beyond it. The world can look like a nation, a city, a neighborhood, or a community. You show up each day, clock in, join meetings, and meet deadlines. Yet there is a part of you that knows your purpose is bigger than your position. You move through systems, but you are not defined by them.

You live with dual citizenship: one foot in the marketplace, the other in divine purpose.

The World System

No company or institution exists in isolation. Every organization, whether corporate, educational, governmental, or entrepreneurial, operates within a larger system. These systems are shaped by the laws, culture, and values of the nation they exist in.

Most of these structures reflect the priorities of society: productivity, profit, and progress more than divine purpose or spiritual grounding. Many industries are designed to fit within the world's framework, not a Kingdom-based one. Their goal is to sustain the world's economy, not necessarily your soul's alignment.

To move wisely through these systems, you must study how they function.

Understanding Without Conforming

Understanding how a company works internally and how it operates within the world around it helps you discern how to move through that space without losing your authenticity or spiritual integrity. Awareness does not require agreement. It means observing how a system functions so you can remain intentional.

Economic systems are human-designed structures that shape behavior, incentives, and outcomes, but they do not determine moral responsibility or personal identity. Understanding how these systems function allows individuals to move through them with wisdom rather than imitation. Awareness makes it possible to participate skillfully without surrendering integrity or conviction (Smith, 1776/2007; Friedman, 1962).

"Be wise as serpents and harmless as doves."

Wisdom does not require you to blend in. It calls you to understand how the environment moves so you can move through it with clarity and peace. Even if a system's practices are legal or widely accepted, they may not resonate with your personal, ethical, or spiritual principles.

History has shown that nations, industries, and institutions often operate in ways that conflict with spiritual truth. The systems we live and work in are man-made, created by people with their own motives and limitations. Awareness allows you to interact with these systems without becoming entangled in them. You can function within structures without letting them shape your identity.

Living "in the world but not of it" means recognizing these differences and choosing integrity over assimilation. It means discerning when something looks good on paper but does not sit well in your spirit. It means honoring conviction over convenience.

Awareness gives you freedom. You can be immersed in the system, studying it, working within it, and even succeeding in it, while staying grounded in your values, your mindset, and your mission.

Integration: Creating Within the System

To influence or transform any space, you must understand both its structure and your own source of power.

Think of it this way: as an artist, you do not need technology to create. Everything you need to create is already within you: your voice, your imagination, your ability to shape genious from raw materials. Yet in today's world, technology is woven into almost everything. So even though technology is not essential to your gift, it often becomes essential to how your gift reaches others.

In the same way, understanding the world's systems allows you to stay visible and relevant without compromising who you are. You do not depend on the system to define your gift. You use the system to position your purpose. The system does not give your work meaning. It simply becomes a vessel for it.

This is what it means to live in the world but not of it. You can engage with the systems around you, whether corporate, creative, educational, or entrepreneurial, while staying rooted in a Kingdom perspective. You can learn the structure, navigate the politics, and influence the culture, all while maintaining a heart that's aligned with God's purpose for you.

When you understand the system you are part of, you gain the wisdom to build your own. You learn to work with discernment, crafting a way of operating that is both separate and adaptable. You become a bridge between divine purpose and earthly structure. That is where true harmony begins, moving fluidly through the world while staying anchored in something greater than it.

Closing Thought

The world's systems are designed by people, and as people we are imperfect, ever-evolving, and often imbalanced. That is why awareness matters. You were created with clarity and intention, yet you also carry the same vulnerabilities and limitations that come with being human. Living in this world but not of it does not mean pretending you are beyond its influence. It means staying awake to it. It means recognizing how systems move, how they shape behavior, and how subtle their pull can be.

Awareness is what keeps you grounded. It helps you move wisely instead of reactively. It protects you from being swept into patterns that do not reflect your values or your purpose. The moment you stop observing, you risk absorbing. The moment you stop paying attention, you risk being shaped by what you were meant to rise above.

You were not called to escape the world. You were called to navigate it with discernment. You are both student and strategist, learning how the system works while building something more intentional within it.

Awareness is your advantage. Wisdom is your protection. And your ability to stay conscious in the midst of the world's movement is what allows you to live from your purpose instead of its pressure.

Nine To Five On the Side

Chapter 4

Chapter Four

Protecting Your Vision

Guard the seed before the world can touch it.

When you are building something meaningful, one of the greatest skills you will ever develop is discernment. Not every voice around you is meant to guide you. Not every suggestion is meant to shape you. And not every opportunity is meant to be yours.

Distraction rarely comes shouting. It often comes softly. It comes packaged in care, in admiration, in curiosity, in opportunities that look helpful but quietly pull you away from your direction.

That is why protecting your vision matters. Before anything takes form in your hands, it takes form in your spirit. That early stage is delicate. It is a seed before roots, a spark before flame, a blueprint before structure. And when others speak into that tender space too soon, even with good intentions, it can distort what God is shaping within you.

Your vision is not a community project. It is a divine assignment entrusted to you first.

Protecting What You Are Growing

Everyone will have an opinion once they sense you are building something. Some will cheer you on. Some will try to direct you. Some will do both. But your calling is not built by committee. Protect your vision the way you would protect a seed planted in soil. Before a seed breaks through the surface, it belongs underground, shielded, nurtured, and hidden.

You do not need universal understanding to move forward.
 You only need clarity about what God has placed in you.

There will be seasons when the most important thing you can do is block out the noise: the chatter, the comparison, the "shoulds" and "coulds." What looks reasonable to someone else may not resonate with the divine instruction guiding you.

Some paths look good on paper yet lead to detours, exhaustion, or disappointment because they were based on human logic rather than spiritual direction.

Discernment is what teaches you the difference.

The Subtle Nature of Distraction

Noise does not always come from critics. Often, it comes from people who care about you. When others begin to see your gifts operating, they naturally offer suggestions about how you should use them. Their intentions are usually good. Their advice may even sound wise. But even loving voices can pull you off course if you are not grounded in your purpose.

No one else can hear what you hear inside. No one else has been entrusted with your unique instruction. Try explaining it. They still won't fully grasp it. And that is not a sign to convince them. It is a reminder to listen inwardly before listening outwardly.

People often will not understand your path until it becomes visible. They won't see the meaning behind your choices until the fruit appears. You cannot expect someone to understand a seed when their eyes are trained only on harvest.

This is why discernment matters. You can honor people's intentions without handing them the steering wheel. Your vision was given to you. Protect it accordingly.

Know Your Model and Stay With It

In business and in life, know the model you are building. Clarity is one of your strongest defenses against confusion. Know your foundation, your mission, your rhythm, the flow of your work, and how you move.

If you are still defining it, take your time. Unfolding slowly is better than fast confusion.

When advice comes, use discernment rather than dismissal. Test every suggestion before you implement it.

> **1. Does it align with my goals and mission?**
> If it doesn't fit the foundation God has given you, it is not for you.

> **2. Will it consume time that could be spent on my original plan?**
> Distraction often wears the disguise of opportunity.

> **3. Is this ambition or divine purpose?**

Ambition pushes. Purpose flows. Ambition seeks recognition. Purpose seeks fulfillment.

These questions create space for clarity before you expand or say yes to something new. Sometimes the loudest yes you can give your calling is saying no to everything that doesn't align with it.

Lessons Learned Through Experience

I have lived this lesson more than once. There were seasons when I let outside voices influence my decisions. The ideas sounded good, logical, profitable, and promising. Yet something inside me hesitated.

I followed those ideas anyway.

Thousands of dollars, years of effort, and endless hours later, I learned the difference between ambition and divine instruction.

When I finally quieted the noise, I saw clearly how easy it is to drift when you allow others to guide what God has given you to steward.

Those experiences were not wasted. They were classrooms. They helped me recognize that the most fruitful ideas are the ones that bring peace, flow naturally, and genuinely help others.

Once I understood that, protecting my vision became non-negotiable.

Beyond Voices: The Noise You See

Noise is not only spoken. Sometimes, it flashes across your screen.

It lives in social media feeds, images, trends, the appearance of success, and the illusion of urgency. Even motivational content can become mental clutter when consumed excessively.

Visual noise can distort your sense of timing. It can convince you that everyone is ahead of you. It can make your pace feel insufficient when, in truth, it is exactly the pace you need.

Guard your eyes as intentionally as you guard your ears.

Silencing digital noise does not require disconnection. It requires discernment. Curate what you see. Limit what drains you. Reduce exposure to content that shifts you away from your authentic path.

Silence as Strategy

Silence carries intention. It offers a moment of grounding and renewal, a precious space where understanding unfolds with greater clarity. In stillness, through listening and reflection, insight emerges and awareness deepens. This quiet attentiveness creates room to perceive divine direction with discernment.

Quiet seasons shouldn't be daunting; they are often where your deepest understanding grows and where the next chapter of your life gathers strength.

Keep It to Yourself Until You're Ready

Momentum is fragile in the early stages of building anything. The fastest way to lose momentum is by sharing too soon.

Your ideas are seeds. They need privacy before exposure. They need grounding before feedback. They need development before discussion.

You are not being secretive. You are being wise. Privacy preserves focus. Privacy protects authenticity. Privacy guards the internal process that others cannot interpret.

People can unintentionally shift your direction with a single comment, question, or opinion. That is why timing matters. Every idea has its season of silence.

The Power of Words

The influence of external words is real. Think about music. Have you ever heard a song or commercial jingle that stayed in your mind all day without permission? Certain melodies or phrases lodge themselves into memory and resurface years later, triggered by a place, a scent, or a moment. That is the power of someone else's words. They linger. They shape mental space. They influence mood, confidence, and decision-making without your consent.

Now imagine sharing your idea, vision, or concept with someone, and they respond with opinions that differ from your own. They may mean well, they may care deeply, but their words can still settle into your thoughts the same way a song does. They replay. They echo. They interrupt the rhythm of your inner guidance.

This is why timing matters. This is why privacy matters. This is why discernment matters.

Opinions from trusted advisors can be valuable, but they should never outweigh the wisdom of your own insight. A single comment can influence how you see your work. A single question can make you hesitate. A single suggestion can seed doubt where there was once clarity.

Your thoughts, your vision, and your plan must have the loudest presence as you build. External voices should never overpower the internal voice that received the instruction in the first place.

Closing Thought

You will always have voices around you. Some helpful. Some distracting. Some genuinely loving. But the only voice with authority to guide your path is the still, small voice within.

It may not shout.
It may not convince others.
But it will always lead you toward peace.

Protect your vision.
Honor the quiet guidance within you.
Guard your pace, your process, and your purpose.

Silence serves as preparation, creating space to gather strength, intention, and focus.

What grows in private will shine in public when the time is right.

Chapter Five

Mastery In Motion

Honoring Your Time and Your Gifts

We are given twenty-four hours each day, and every hour is a seed. The choices you make within those moments influence what grows in your life tomorrow.

This chapter is not about time management. It is about purpose stewardship. It is about realizing that the hours you spend in your current environment are not wasted moments. They are training grounds. They are shaping you for where you are going, whether you recognize it or not.

Growth does not wait for convenience. Purpose does not pause until your schedule opens. Your preparation season is not a future moment. It is happening right now, every day, in the middle of responsibilities, deadlines, and ordinary routines.

You do not need to escape your current environment to begin becoming who you are called to be. You can build while you work.

The Myth of "When I Have Time"

The most dangerous lie you can tell yourself is that your purpose must wait for a quieter season.

"When things slow down, I'll start."
"When I leave this job, I'll finally pursue my dream."
"When life settles, I'll have time."

But time does not slow down. Time responds to intention. The same twenty-four hours that overwhelm you today could build you tomorrow if you learn to see them through a different lens.

You do not find time. You make time. And in the making, you make yourself.

Every day holds opportunities for discipline, clarity, and self-awareness. The difference is how intentional you are with what is already in your hands. When you treat time as a tool rather than something to survive, you stop enduring your day and begin shaping it.

Your Environment Is Your Gym

Your current environment, whether corporate, educational, healthcare, or entrepreneurial, is your training ground. Every project, every conversation, every challenge is an exercise in character development. Your workplace is not just where you earn; it's where you learn.

If you pay attention, you'll notice how each experience builds something internal. Every meeting tests your patience. Every difficult client strengthens your communication skills. Every setback stretches your endurance. You're developing while working.

When you begin to view your workplace as training rather than confinement, frustration transforms into clarity. You learn what needs strengthening, what needs shifting, and what needs letting go. *Are you reactive or reflective under pressure? Do you advocate for your ideas, or do you shrink when challenged? Do you move authentically, or for approval?*

These questions are not meant to convict, they're meant to clarify. Because your current environment is not your limitation. It's your gym.

Audit Your 24

To grow while you work, you must know where your time is going. Audit your hours honestly. Not just your schedule, but your energy. What drains you? What feeds you? Where are you over giving? Where are you withholding your best effort?

Awareness is the first step to alignment. You cannot steward what you will not examine.

When you map out your hours, you begin to see patterns. You start noticing where your purpose is calling for more focus and where distraction has taken root.

Leave Work at Work

Building something meaningful requires mental space. You will be challenged to give your attention to your purpose if your mind is still carrying the weight of your workday. This often shows up as replaying conflicts from the day or carrying the emotional weight of responsibilities that do not belong to you once you walk out the door.

This is not about being careless with your job. It is about refusing to let your job consume the mental space your purpose needs to grow.

Too many people never activate their vision because work follows them home, not on paper, but in thought. They carry unfinished tasks, imaginary arguments, the pressure to prove themselves, or the emotional residue of those who require more than they can give.

You will be challenged in pursuing your potential if you are mentally employed 24/7.

Give your job your excellence during the hours you are paid, not your evenings, not your weekends, not your dreams.

Build While You Work

Building while you work is not about adding more tasks. It's about changing your posture and deciding to show up differently, even in the same environment.

You can still dream while you meet deadlines. You can still build vision as you honor your job. You simply need to learn to show up differently.

The same qualities that will make you successful in your business (consistency, empathy, clarity, and discipline) can be cultivated right where you are.

Use your one-on-one meetings to practice active listening. Turn your lunch breaks into moments for journaling or prayer. Use your commute to feed your mind with wisdom and insight. Volunteer for projects that challenge your leadership muscles.

When you begin to see your current environment as part of your preparation, frustration turns into gratitude. You start building from within and that's where lasting growth begins.

The Bridge Into Mastery

Once you learn to steward your time, your next step is mastery.

Mastery is about becoming so aligned with your work that it flows through you naturally. It's about learning deeply enough that skill becomes second nature, not through force, but through steady, intentional repetition. Research on skill development shows that mastery is formed through deliberate, focused practice over time, with growth emerging through intentional repetition and gradual refinement (Ericsson & Pool, 2016).

The goal is not simply to perform tasks but to internalize understanding. To reach the point where what once required effort now moves through you with ease. Mastery is what transforms repetition into rhythm and discipline into grace.

Why Mastery Matters

Mastery is important for two main reasons: **capacity** and **credibility.**

Capacity

Mastery expands your ability to hold more. When you've fully learned one level, you're prepared to receive greater knowledge, skill, and responsibility. Each level of mastery lays the foundation for the next. It is a process of progression; precept upon precept, lesson upon lesson.

For example, you will be challenged in managing others effectively if you haven't learned to manage yourself. Mastery strengthens your foundation so you can carry more without collapsing under the weight of what you are building.

Even in an ever-changing world where technology advances and systems evolve, mastery still matters. The act of mastering one thing trains your mind and spirit to adapt to the next. Every new innovation, challenge, or opportunity becomes easier to navigate once you've learned the discipline of mastery.

The habit of mastery sharpens your focus, builds endurance, and strengthens your ability to stay relevant no matter how much the world evolves.

Credibility

Mastery becomes your record; your reputation and silent advocate.

Mastery also builds credibility that outlasts any position or company. Every season of employment becomes part of your professional record. The skills you refine, the reputation you build, and the results you deliver all speak on your behalf.

Most organizations measure growth through reviews, evaluations, or reports that assess consistency, effectiveness, and leadership potential. Those records do more than serve the company; they serve you. They become part of your professional identity and your personal brand.

So when you transition into a new role, a new industry, or even into entrepreneurship, that record speaks for you. It testifies to your discipline, your integrity, and your excellence.

Mastery is what verifies your credibility when others speak your name.

> *"Do everything with such excellence that when your name is mentioned, your work defends you."*

The Discipline of Repetition

Repetition is where mastery lives. The daily, often unseen practice of doing something repeatedly, refining it, noticing what feels off, and improving. It is what separates growth from performance.

The more you repeat with awareness, the deeper your understanding becomes. Mastery requires presence. It's not about mechanical repetition but about conscious refinement.

Every job task, conversation, or project is a chance to practice something at a deeper level, whether it's patience, leadership, clarity, or creativity. Your workplace becomes a living classroom.

When you use your current environment as a training ground, you transform ordinary moments into opportunities for mastery.

Forward Thinking While You Work

Even when you're working under someone else's vision, remember that you're still building your own. Each project or task is part of your preparation for what's ahead.

You're not just mastering a job; you're mastering yourself as well as your responses, your standards, your habits, and your ability to follow through.

Mastery today builds the foundation for leadership tomorrow. It ensures that when your next opportunity arrives, you have both the skill and the character to sustain it.

Forward thinking is about seeing beyond the task to the transformation. You are becoming the kind of person who can carry the weight of your next level.

The Inner Work of Mastery

There is an inner rhythm to mastery, a quiet connection between your diligence and divine timing. Scripture teaches that "to whom much is given, much is required." Mastery is the process of becoming trustworthy with what is already in your hands so that you can be trusted with more.

As you sharpen your skills, you are also shaping your spirit, developing patience, humility, endurance, and the maturity needed to carry greater responsibility.

Transferable Mastery

Once a skill is mastered, it doesn't stay confined to the environment where it was learned. Mastery becomes a transferable strength, something you can carry with you into any new context, career, or calling.

When you've developed discipline, patience, communication, or leadership, those qualities don't disappear when your title or workplace changes. They move with you. They show up in how you handle challenges, how you lead others, and how you build what's next.

For example, a person who once managed teams in a corporate office can later lead a business because the same principles apply: vision, structure, and accountability. An educator can evolve into a coach or trainer because teaching is not limited to classrooms; it's a skill of communication and transformation. Or an administrative assistant can transition into entrepreneurship because their mastery of organization and foresight becomes the foundation for building systems that sustain growth.

When skill evolves into character, it goes with you into every space you enter.

That's the essence of transferable mastery; the skills you sharpen in one space become the visible strengths that elevate you in new spaces.

Closing Thought

Mastery is both discipline and declaration.

You declare readiness by refining what is already in your hands. You build capacity by finishing what you start. You gain credibility by doing it well. And you strengthen your future by honoring your present.

The world's systems will always evolve; tools will change, industries will shift, and methods will transform. But mastery gives you the agility to evolve with them.

Before you are trusted with more, you must be faithful with what is in your care today.

Mastery is your preparation for the next dimension of your purpose.

Chapter 6

Chapter Six

Delayed Gratification

Stay committed even when progress feels invisible.

There's a kind of work that doesn't show up in numbers, likes, or applause. It's the work of consistency and showing up when no one's watching. It is the quiet work beneath the surface; planting seeds without knowing exactly when they'll bloom.

Delayed gratification is not just a discipline; it's a mindset. It's the ability to keep going when results are slow, feedback is quiet, and the path feels uncertain. It's trusting that what you're building matters, even when it's not yet visible.

Think of a seed underground. It's growing, stretching, rooting, and no one sees it. The soil is dark, the process is hidden, but the transformation is real. That's what your journey looks like in seasons of delayed gratification.

In these hidden seasons, it's not that nothing is happening; it's that everything is happening beneath the surface. The foundation is forming. The unseen work is preparing you for what's to come.

The Temptation to Quit

We live in a world that rewards speed, visibility, and instant success. It is easy to look around, see others launching or celebrating, and assume your slow progress means you are falling behind.

But comparison is a thief of timing. Your process has its own divine rhythm. The work you're doing now, though quiet, steady, and unseen, is laying the foundation for something lasting.

You are not behind. You are unfolding.

Every moment of endurance strengthens you. Every act of patience shapes your character. Every step you take, no matter how small, brings you closer to the vision you have been entrusted with.

Reframing Progress

True progress shows up when you say no to distraction and yes to what resonates with your purpose. It is choosing rest when your body needs recovery, not forcing yourself into exhaustion. It is refining your message until it feels true to your voice, deepening your character, and remaining faithful to the process even when you cannot yet see the outcome.

These moments support development, reinforcing the roots that will eventually bear fruit. When you redefine progress, you reclaim peace in your process.

The Power of Waiting Well

There is a well-known study where children were given a simple choice. They could receive a small reward immediately, or they could wait for a period of time and receive something greater. The environment was intentionally quiet. No encouragement was offered. The children were left alone with the decision (Mischel, 2014).

What the study revealed over time was not about willpower or intelligence. It revealed how people relate to discomfort, desire, and waiting.

Some children struggled not because they lacked discipline, but because waiting created uncertainty. Sitting with the unknown felt harder than accepting what was immediately available. Others learned to redirect their attention. They sang, looked away, talked to themselves, or found ways to stay focused on something beyond the reward in front of them.

The difference was not the reward. It was the ability to endure the pause.

This mirrors the reality of delayed gratification in business. The challenge is rarely about effort. It is about remaining steady when there is no immediate confirmation that your work is paying off. It is about resisting the urge to reach for quick relief when long-term impact requires patience.

Protecting Your Commitment

Delayed gratification requires emotional endurance. It asks you to believe in what you cannot yet see, to have faith in the unseen, and to protect that belief like something precious. This is where the work from Chapter Three becomes essential. When we explored the importance of protecting your vision and blocking out the noise, it was not just about guarding ideas; it was about safeguarding the strength you will need during seasons when progress feels slow.

Times of delay make you more vulnerable to outside influence. Doubt grows louder when results are quiet. This is why your ability to block out noise is not optional; it is part of your survival. To sustain your momentum, you must be intentional about the voices and environments that shape your thoughts. Guard your mind from discouragement. Surround yourself with people who honor your process, not people who rush it or redefine it for you.

Celebrate even the smallest victories, not because they are grand, but because they are signs of movement. Keep your focus on the long game rather than the momentary metrics the world uses to measure success.

Your commitment is a reflection of your faith. Every time you choose patience over panic and focus over frenzy, you strengthen the foundation beneath you. Delayed seasons refine endurance and strengthen purpose over time.

Closing Thought

You are not waiting; you are working.
You are not stuck; you are being strengthened.
The results may be delayed, but the impact will be undeniable.
Stay committed, stay faithful, and stay rooted. The harvest is coming.

"Let perseverance finish its work so that you may be mature and complete, not lacking anything."

TaKenya White

Chapter 7

Chapter Seven

Purposeful Connections

Building a Network That Supports Growth

Before you can connect outwardly, you must be anchored inwardly. Purposeful connections are born from clarity, mastery, and the careful protection of your vision. In a world that often confuses networking with visibility, it is easy to believe you must be everywhere to make progress. But true expansion does not begin with exposure. It begins with discernment.

You don't need to be in every room. You need to be in the right ones. You need people, spaces, and opportunities that reflect where you are growing, not just where you have been.

This chapter is not about collecting contacts. It is about cultivating relationships with intention, expanding wisely, and building a network that strengthens the integrity of what you have already begun.

From Solitude to Strategy

Every meaningful network begins in solitude. Solitude is the season where your voice strengthens, your purpose clarifies, and your confidence deepens. It is where you protect your vision, develop your skills, and refine the work that will one day speak on your behalf.

Once the foundation is formed, connection becomes the next step. Not because you need validation, but because your work is ready to be shared. Networking is not the abandonment of solitude. It is the extension of it.

When you step into professional spaces, you are not showing up to prove yourself. You are showing up prepared. Solitude taught you discernment. Networking allows you to move with that discernment in real time.

You do not need every connection. You need the connections that fit your mission.

The Right Time to Network

Timing matters. Just as a seed is not planted in every season, your work should not be shared in every environment.

Before stepping into new circles, take a moment to ground yourself in what you know. Be sure that your ideas are clear enough to communicate naturally, that your work is protected and documented, and that you are entering new spaces from a place of confidence rather than a desire for validation.

These internal checkpoints keep you anchored as you expand outward. When you move with that kind of clarity, you naturally attract people who understand your direction and honor the pace you are growing in.

The people and organizations meant for your next level will not require you to shrink or stretch beyond integrity just to fit. They will meet you in purpose, not pressure.

The Purpose of Networking

Networking is the exchange of value, information, and opportunity. It is how you gain visibility, insight, and access in ways that strengthen your assignment. It is how your work enters new rooms and reaches the people it is meant to impact.

Networking is relational. It grows through connection, shared values, mutual respect, and thoughtful intention.

The right network helps you to gain perspective, strengthen your professional identity, expand into new opportunities, refine your voice and ideas, and connect with those who can speak your name in rooms you have not yet entered.

The focus is on connection with those who strengthen your purpose, support it, and grow beside it.

Quality Over Quantity in Professional Circles

A vast network is different from a purposeful one. What matters is not how many people you know, but how deeply your connections support your development.

Every type of connection has purpose.

Mentors challenge you to rise higher. They offer wisdom, perspective, and correction. Peers collaborate and exchange insight. They walk beside you, sharing the weight and wonder of the journey.
Allies advocate for your presence in rooms you're not yet in. They speak your name in spaces you haven't entered.
Mentees remind you that legacy is a cycle, not a destination. They keep you grounded in purpose and generous with your wisdom.

Each relationship type plays a different role, but all require intentionality. Choose people who reflect integrity, reciprocity, and respect.

Networking with Discernment

Discernment is just as important in professional spaces as it is in personal relationships. Not every opportunity aligns with your mission, and not every connection is meant to follow you into the next season of growth.

As you meet new people, allow yourself to notice how the interaction feels. Consider whether the connection strengthens your confidence, aligns with your values, or expands your perspective in meaningful ways.

Aligned professional connections help you think deeper and move smarter. They inspire new ideas, sharpen your skills, and strengthen your confidence.

Misaligned connections pull you into spaces that drain your energy, blur your vision, or pressure you to perform.

You are not obligated to participate in every conversation or accept every invitation. Discernment protects your energy, your reputation, and your purpose.

Protecting Your Vision While You Network

Networking requires openness; that doesn't mean full exposure. Share your enthusiasm without revealing your entire blueprint. Introduce your work without unveiling your full process.

Protecting your vision is the wisdom of knowing when to reveal, when to withhold, and when to wait. Every purpose has timing, and every idea has a season.

You don't have to share every detail or defend your value to anyone. It is both wise and appropriate to protect what is still developing until it is strong enough to stand on its own.

Showing Up with Purpose

When entering professional spaces, let purpose guide your presence. You do not need to impress anyone. You need to be authentic, prepared, and grounded in your assignment.

Show up with integrity, consistency, excellence, and humility. Allow your character, preparation, and work ethic to introduce you before you speak. The reputation formed through mastery, humility, and faith becomes its own advocate.

A steady, grounded presence often creates more meaningful impact than constant visibility. Be mindful of this; you are not marketing yourself. You are making yourself available to the right people, in the right places, at the right time.

Spiritual Guidance in Networking

Even in professional settings, discernment and spiritual awareness matter. Every connection carries influence. Not every space is meant for you.

As you navigate new circles, ask for guidance in the way that resonates with your faith. I pray as I move through new environments, trusting that clarity and peace will reveal what aligns and what does not. Pay attention to the inner cues that help you sense intention. Look beyond charisma and notice character. Aligned connections will elevate your purpose, while misaligned ones can drain your progress.

Discernment leads you toward opportunities that are purposeful rather than distracting.

Closing Thought

You build alone so you can connect with clarity.
You connect wisely so you can expand with integrity.

Every season of growth requires new relationships, but wisdom teaches you to discern who is for this season and who is for the next.

When you are rooted in purpose, connection becomes less about being seen and more about being sent.

CHAPTER 8

CHAPTER EIGHT

PERSONAL FINANCES

Creating Habits That Support Long-Term Success
Featuring "Financial Foundations from a CPA's Perspective" by Aleicha Addison

Personal finances are not separate from purpose. They are part of how you honor what you are called to build. A business can be fueled by talent and vision, but without financial discipline, it struggles to stand. Even the strongest dream can wobble under the weight of unmanaged money.

Think of your financial life as the grounding beneath your work. When you understand how your money moves, you gain clarity. When you handle it wisely, you gain peace. When you prepare for growth, you create room for expansion.

You do not need to be perfect with numbers to be responsible with them. What matters most is awareness and consistency. The habits you build now will support the freedom you desire later.

Take it from me. Choose to be wise with your finances. Wisdom in this area protects your purpose, steadies your decisions, and strengthens your foundation as you rise. It is a form of stewardship, a way of saying, I honor what has been placed in my hands.

Start Smart, Even Without a Full-Time Accountant

Most beginners do not start with a full financial team, and that is perfectly fine. What matters in the early stages is not having everything but understanding the basics of what you have.

Begin by separating your personal and business finances. Open a dedicated business account as soon as possible. This simple step keeps your books clean, builds credibility, and helps you see your progress without confusion.

Track your income and expenses each month. Even if you hire someone to assist you later, consistency now strengthens your future decisions. Today, tools such as *QuickBooks, Expensify, Wave*, and *FreshBooks* support this process by organizing receipts, tracking mileage, categorizing expenses, and exporting clear reports with ease.

Think of financial tracking as self-awareness for your business. You cannot grow what you do not measure. When you stay connected to your numbers, you stay connected to your direction.

Small, steady habits create confidence. The more intentional you become, the more prepared you are when greater opportunities begin to flow.

Understand the Basics Before You Delegate

Even when you eventually hire an accountant or bookkeeper, your responsibility does not disappear. Delegation is support, not surrender. You still remain the steward of your financial decisions.

Before you hand anything over, learn the essentials. Know your income streams, your recurring expenses, and the categories your transactions fall into. Review your reports regularly and ask questions, even the ones that feel too small or too simple. Your understanding is part of your protection.

There have been many situations where finances were mishandled because the owner trusted the process but never learned the basics. The lesson is simple. You can assign tasks, but you cannot release your accountability.

When you understand your numbers, you walk into every decision with authority. This clarity strengthens your confidence and ensures that your future is guided by insight, not assumption. Stewardship begins with awareness.

Understanding Taxes on Your Business Income

Taxes are not a surprise; they should not feel mysterious or frightening. Taxes are simply part of how the financial system functions. When you prepare early, you protect your peace later.

If you work a traditional job, your employer already withholds federal taxes, Social Security, and Medicare. That portion is handled.

But the moment you start earning money outside of your job, through a service, selling products, consulting, or any alternative income stream, you enter a new category. This income is treated as self-employment income, and you are responsible for setting a portion aside for taxes (Internal Revenue Service, n.d.; U.S. Department of the Treasury, n.d.).

This is where many new entrepreneurs feel caught off guard, but it does not have to be stressful. Understanding the system allows you to plan, not panic.

Most beginning entrepreneurs fall within these income ranges:
Less than one hundred thousand dollars for individuals
Less than two hundred thousand dollars for married couples filing jointly (Internal Revenue Service, n.d.).

These ranges help identify the tax bracket that most new business owners fall into and provide a simple foundation for calculating what to reserve.

As a point of awareness, research shows the mean annual income in 2026 is around sixty-five to seventy thousand dollars, with modest growth each year. This helps you understand the financial landscape you are building in and plan with a long-term perspective (Bureau of Labor Statistics, n.d.; Bureau of Economic Analysis, n.d.).

The principle is simple. When new income enters your life, treat it with intention. Assign a portion of it to taxes, and you create stability instead of surprise.

The Simple Formula

When you earn business or alternative income, the simplest way to stay prepared is to set aside a percentage of what you make. This keeps you from feeling overwhelmed during tax season and helps you build healthy financial habits from the beginning.

A reliable starting point is to reserve twenty-five to thirty percent of your business income (Internal Revenue Service, n.d.; U.S. Small Business Administration, n.d.). This percentage does not apply to your W-2 salary from your job. It applies only to the money you earn through your business or side work.

To make this feel familiar, let's revisit a classic math *word problem* from elementary school for a moment.

Imagine that White Plumbing Company LLC earned **$2,000** per month in its first year of business. If we multiply the company's monthly income by the standard tax-reserve rate of **30%**, how much should the company set aside for **tax reserves** each month?

The formula looks like this:

$$\text{Monthly Income} \times 0.30 = \text{Tax Reserves}$$
$$\$2{,}000 \times 0.30 = \$600$$

When we apply it:

White Plumbing Company LLC should place six hundred dollars each month into a separate tax savings account. This practice builds discipline. It prepares the business for federal income tax, self-employment tax, and any small adjustments that may occur. This is financial stewardship in action. When you prepare well, you create room for your business to grow with ease. You remove the emotional weight that often comes with tax season because the structure is already in place.

Every seed of discipline you plant now becomes stability for your future.

Paying Yourself Wisely

Many entrepreneurs struggle with knowing when, and how much, to pay themselves. The reality is, there is no single formula that works for everyone. What matters most is understanding your season and creating habits that support long-term stability.

Before we walk through the numbers, it helps to set a realistic baseline. In 2026, the average annual income in the United States is approximately sixty to seventy thousand dollars a year. For the purpose of planning, this chapter uses one hundred thousand dollars as a goal-based projection. It gives you a wider view of what your income could look like as your business grows.

A simple way to think about your earning potential is this: *Entrepreneurial Income = $100,000 – (Your 9-to-5 Income)*

This formula is not a rule. It is a vision tool. It helps you see how your business income may evolve over time.

In the early stage, it may be best to reinvest most profits rather than paying yourself a full salary (U.S. Small Business Administration, n.d.; USA.gov, n.d.). This allows the business to grow its foundation, build systems, and stay financially healthy. Reinvesting also lowers your tax burden because you are keeping more funds inside the business where they can work for you.

The goal for your first one to two years is sustainability. As your structure becomes stronger and your income becomes more consistent, you can gradually increase what you pay yourself. Think of it as creating a flow that supports both your personal life and your long-term business vision.

Below is a simple visual guide to help you think about income distribution. It gives you an idea of how taxes, reinvestment, and take-home pay might look based on different earning situations. These numbers are only reference points. They are not expectations.

Visual Example: Pay Yourself Wisely

Filing Status	9-to-5 Income	Projected Entrepreneurial Income	Suggested Tax Withholding (25–30%)	Suggested Reinvestment (20–30%)	Approx. Take-Home Pay
Single	$60,000	$40,000	$10,000–$12,000	$8,000–$12,000	$16,000–$22,000
Married (Joint)	$75,000	$25,000	$6,250–$7,500	$5,000–$7,500	$10,000–$12,500
Head of Household	$50,000	$50,000	$12,500–$15,000	$10,000–$15,000	$20,000–$25,000

If you earn $65,000 at your job, your entrepreneurial target is $35,000. This strategy supports gradual growth, minimizes tax liability, and strengthens long-term sustainability.

If possible, delay paying yourself during the early stages. Growth always requires seed before harvest. When you focus on strengthening your systems first, you give your business the freedom to expand without strain.

When You're Already Earning Well

If your 9-to-5 income already exceeds $100,000, your strategy shifts from survival to stewardship. Think like an investor. Let your business income work for you, fund growth, expand opportunities, and strengthen long-term freedom.

When you are already earning well, the way you use your business income matters just as much as the amount you receive. The goal is not to increase lifestyle spending simply because more money is coming in. The goal is to create structure that keeps your business healthy and your future flexible.

A simple and effective approach is to:

- Pay yourself **10 to 20%** of your business profit
- Reinvest **40 to 50%**
- Reserve **25 to 30%** for taxes
- Save whatever remains as business cushion

This creates a rhythm that keeps your business stable. Structure supports longevity.

Numerical Example

Now let's look a scenario where White Plumbing Company LLC is now earning **$15,000 per month**.

The owner decides to follow this plan:

- **15%** for personal pay
- **45%** for reinvestment
- **30%** for taxes

Here is what that looks like:

1. Pay to Self: $15,000 × 0.15 = **$2,250**

2. Reinvestment: $15,000 × 0.45 = **$6,750**

3. Tax Reserve: $15,000 × 0.30 = **$4,500**

4. Remaining Business Savings: $15,000 − ($2,250 + $6,750 + $4,500) = **$1,500**

If White Plumbing Company LLC earns $15,000 per month, its recommended breakdown is:

Final Monthly Breakdown:
- **$2,250 — Pay to Self**
- **$6,750 — Reinvestment**
- **$4,500 — Tax Reserve**
- **$1,500 — Business Savings**

When every dollar has an assignment, your business becomes more stable.

This is only one example of how an entrepreneur might structure their monthly income, but seeing the numbers laid out visually creates clarity. It helps you avoid overspending, prepare for growth, make decisions from intention rather than panic, and maintain liquidity that supports peace of mind.

This level of stewardship strengthens long-term sustainability. It allows your business to expand without creating financial strain and positions you to move with confidence when new opportunities arise.

Looking Ahead: Tax Trends and Future Planning

Financial clarity isn't just about the present; it's also about preparing for the future. Taxes, laws, and economic patterns shift over time, and the more informed you are, the more confidently you can make long-term decisions.

History offers valuable insight. Over the last 30 years, income tax rates have generally increased across the United States, rising an average of **1 to 3% per decade** (U.S. Department of the Treasury, n.d.; Federal Reserve System, n.d.). If this pattern continues, it's reasonable to expect similar increases by **2036**. This projection isn't meant to create fear; it's meant to help you plan wisely.

Long-term entrepreneurs don't simply react to financial changes; they prepare for them. When you build your business with a forward-thinking mindset, you protect your growth from unexpected changes.

You don't need to become an expert in tax law; I'm simply suggesting that you review current tax rates each year, maintain a steady habit of saving and reserving funds, adjust your strategy as your income changes, and seek professional guidance when necessary. Thinking ahead ensures that your success is not just built, but sustained.

Your future stability will depend not only on how much you earn, but on how consistently you prepare for what's ahead. Financial stewardship grows your capacity by keeping you informed, grounded, and ready for whatever season comes next.

Choosing a Business Structure

The structure you choose for your business determines how you pay taxes, how you protect your personal assets, and how you report your income. Many people overcomplicate this part of entrepreneurship, but you don't have to. You are not choosing a lifelong identity; you are choosing the structure that fits the season you're in.

The goal is not to start big. The goal is to start right.

In the early building phase, a **Sole Proprietorship** is often the most practical starting point. It offers simple setup and direct control, allowing you to focus on building your foundation without administrative complexity.

As you begin growing, hiring help, or expanding your services, transitioning into a Limited Liability Company, often referred to as **LLC,** provides personal protection and clearer tax management, giving you a stronger legal and financial framework.

When your business becomes more established and your revenue increases, an **S-Corporation** can offer greater tax efficiency and payroll flexibility, allowing you to operate with more structure and long-term financial strategy.

Each stage has its own benefits and flow. Choosing the right structure at the right time helps your business grow with integrity and purpose. (Internal Revenue Service, n.d.; U.S. Small Business Administration, n.d.)

Stewardship and Simplicity

Finances can feel intimidating, especially if numbers are not your natural comfort zone. But financial wisdom isn't about perfection; it's about consistency. Small, steady actions create long-term stability.

Stewardship is not about doing everything perfectly. It's about honoring what's in your hands with intention. When you develop simple habits early, you create a financial foundation that supports growth rather than restricts it.

Make it a practice to review your books each month so you can see what's going out, what's coming in, and what needs to be adjusted. Schedule quarterly check-ins with your accountant or advisor to stay on top of changes and prevent surprises. Keep your receipts and financial records organized digitally to make tax season smoother. And remember this simple principle: save first, spend second.

These habits may seem small, but they protect your peace and strengthen your confidence. Financial stewardship is part of divine order. It reflects discipline, clarity, and trust.

"The plans of the diligent lead surely to abundance, but everyone who is hasty comes only to poverty."

These words aren't meant to scare you; they remind you that abundance is often the result of steady, thoughtful preparation.

TaKenya White

NINE TO FIVE ON THE SIDE

FINANCIAL FOUNDATIONS

FROM A CPA'S PERSPECTIVE

By Aleicha Addison, CPA

As a child, I used to count the money in my dad's wallet every day. I didn't do it because I was nosy - I did it because I wanted to understand how he spent his money. Thankfully, he was willing to explain the choices he made throughout his day for himself and for our family, and how those decisions caused the amount of money to rise or fall. That is how I learned stewardship.

When you are a faithful steward over your finances, you don't fear sharing your plans and decisions with others. You simply learn to use wisdom - knowing who is assigned to be an advisor in your life and who is simply being nosy. But one truth remains: good stewardship is always the result of good accountability.

Find someone you trust to share your financial health with consistently. Not only when you're earning money, but especially when you're facing hard times and difficult financial choices. There is safety in the multitude of counsel.

The biggest advice I give every new entrepreneur who asks, "What should I be most concerned about?" is this: integrity. Be integral with your finances. Give to Caesar what is Caesar's. Crawl before you jump. Make wise, long-term decisions for yourself and your business. Find a way to give back to the community. And always seek sound counsel.

Closing Thought

This chapter is not meant to overwhelm you; it's meant to prepare you. Financial wisdom is not about how much you have, but how faithfully you manage what's in your hands. When you understand your numbers and create structure around them, you build more than income; you build stability, freedom, and legacy.

A successful business is built with intention, clarity, and responsibility. Knowing how to handle your finances is part of that integrity. You are building income, stability, freedom, and legacy.

CHAPTER 9

Chapter Nine

You Are a Service Provider

Shift Your Identity from Employee to Empowered Entrepreneur

Language Shapes Identity

The way you speak about your work reflects how you see yourself. When you call yourself *just an employee*, you reinforce limitation. When you say *I'm building something*, you activate ownership.

You are not working *for* a company, organization, or institution; you are working *with* them. You were hired because of who you are and what you bring. Your ideas, your skill set, and your unique way of approaching problems are part of the value you offer. You are already providing a service, and no one can deliver that service the way you do. Even if someone fills your role after you leave, they will not bring your voice or your perspective.

Entrepreneurship begins with language. Before there are business cards, websites, or LLCs, there is a shift in how you speak about what you do. You are not just completing tasks or clocking in for hours; you are offering solutions, creating value, and serving through your gifts.

From Employee to Entrepreneur

This shift in language is not about quitting your job; it's about changing your posture. You can be employed and still operate as a service provider. You can work within a system and still build something of your own.

When you begin to see yourself as a business, everything changes. Employees wait for direction, but service providers create solutions. Employees clock in for time, but entrepreneurs show up with purpose. Employees seek permission, but entrepreneurs move with clarity and intention.

The shift begins when you stop saying, *"I work for this company,"* and start saying, *"I serve through this organization."* It deepens when you stop asking, *"what do they want from me?"* and start asking, *"what impact am I making?"*

Every task becomes an opportunity to practice excellence. Every challenge becomes a chance to refine your craft. Every project becomes part of your portfolio of service. You are not being used by a company; you are collaborating with it to exchange value.

Your Work Is a Service

Every skill you have developed, every insight you have gained, and every solution you have offered is part of your service. Whether you are a strategist, educator, healer, artist, builder, or creator of any kind, your work carries weight.

You are not simply doing a job. You are offering transformation. You are not filling a role. You are fulfilling a purpose.

Once you see yourself as a service provider, your confidence shifts. Your language becomes clearer. Your decisions become more intentional. You begin to recognize that the same excellence you offer an employer can be directed toward your own business. Ancient wisdom traditions have long framed work and commerce as forms of service and responsibility, teaching that value is created through contribution, integrity, and care for others rather than position alone (Brackman, 2009).

The skills that help an organization grow can help your calling grow. The discipline that sustains a company can sustain your vision.

You are already in business. The company you work *with* is simply one of your clients.

Power, Love, and Sound Judgment

It may feel uncomfortable to shift into this mindset but remember:

"God has not given us a spirit of fear, but one of power and love and sound judgement."

This truth is more than encouragement. It is a blueprint for how you show up. You are not designed to operate in fear or smallness. You were created to lead with power, serve with love, and build with steady, grounded judgment.

Your identity is rooted in power, not passivity. You are equipped to speak with confidence and move with assurance. What you carry cannot be diminished by a title, confined by a job, or defined by an institution.

Change Your Language

Words matter. They shape your perception and guide your actions. Begin speaking from a place of ownership, not obligation.

Instead of saying, *"I'm trying to start something,"* say, *"I'm building solutions,"* or *"I run a service-based business."* Instead of saying, *"I hope it works,* say, *I'm committed to serving well."*

This isn't about exaggeration or ego; it's about faith in what you are purposed to do. Your words should match your intentions. When your language aligns with your purpose, your actions begin to follow.

The Power of Posture

When you change your language, you change your posture. You walk differently. You present differently. You attract differently. Clients and collaborators respond to confidence. Opportunities respond to ownership.

You don't have to be loud to be clear, and you don't have to be flashy to be credible. You simply need to speak from the truth of who you are and the service you provide.

Closing Thought

You are not just working. You are serving. You are not just employed. You are empowered. You are not working *for* an organization. You are working *with* it, offering value in exchange for opportunity.

Change your language, and your identity will evolve.
Change your identity, and your future will open.

You are a service provider. Build from that truth.

Chapter 10

Chapter Ten

Partnerships

Collaborate Wisely and Intentionally

Not every connection becomes a partnership. Networking introduces you to possibilities, but partnership brings you into accountability. It is where vision meets agreement, and where the stakes become higher. Partnership is not a casual handshake. It is a shared commitment. It is the moment when your private work begins to merge with someone else's rhythm, values, and intentions. This chapter is not about collaboration for convenience; it is about collaboration with conviction.

Partnerships require discernment and discipline. You are not just combining skills; you are intertwining systems, strategies, and spirits. You are choosing to build with someone who will touch what you have protected, speak into what you have refined, and walk beside what you have developed in solitude. That is not light work.

Partnership Is Divine

Partnership is not just collaboration; it is covenant. When you choose to build with someone, you are not simply sharing tasks. You are sharing trust, timing, and territory. You are inviting someone to enter the protected space of your vision and to co-steward it with you.

This is why partnership must be chosen with wisdom rather than urgency, with discernment instead of desperation, and with clarity rather than charm or enthusiasm. You do not partner with someone because they are available. You partner because they are aligned.

Partnership is not just about skill. It is about who someone is when no one is watching. It is about how they handle pressure, honor boundaries, and respond to correction. It is about character, not just competence.

A person with exceptional talent but poor integrity can unravel years of work. A creative collaborator with no consistency can disrupt momentum. A well-intentioned friend without an understanding of professional boundaries can compromise your vision. Choose wisely.

The Difference Between Help and Partnership

Not everyone who offers help is meant to be a partner. Some people are assigned to support you for a season; others are called to build with you for the long term.

Help is transactional. Partnership is transformational.

Help says, *"I will assist you."* Partnership says, *"I will invest in this with you."* Help shows up for the task. Partnership shows up for the vision.

Before you agree to collaborate, consider whether you are aligned in values or only in skills. Reflect on whether you share a vision or simply share a goal. Notice if the person is committed to the process rather than just the outcome. And pay close attention to whether you feel spiritually grounded or emotionally pressured.

Protecting Your Vision in Partnership

Partnership requires openness but not exposure. You can collaborate without compromising, and you can share without surrendering.

Protecting your vision includes clear boundaries around roles, expectations, and responsibilities. Put agreements in writing and avoid relying on verbal commitments. Use NDAs when appropriate, even with people you trust. Communicate with honesty and humility. Listen for spiritual confirmation rather than emotional urgency.

No matter how strong a relationship may be, business must be handled professionally. Contracts protect both purpose and peace. They honor the work and prevent confusion.

You are not obligated to partner with people who admire your work. Admiration does not equal assignment. Chemistry is not covenant.

Your vision is precious. Treat it accordingly. You can be kind and still be clear. You can be generous and still be guarded. You can be open and still be wise. Stewardship is not stinginess; it is strategy.

Signs of Aligned Partnership

Aligned partners do more than agree with you; they sharpen you. They challenge your blind spots, honor boundaries, and stretch your capacity.

An aligned partnership is built on shared values, mutual respect, complementary strengths, and clear communication. It reflects emotional maturity, spiritual integrity, and a willingness to grow together rather than simply winning together. It is rooted in commitment to the process, not just the results.

Aligned partners amplify your voice rather than compete with it. They protect your process rather than rush it. They multiply your energy rather than drain it.

They ask questions that deepen your thinking. They offer feedback that strengthens your conviction. They share the weight of the work, not just the celebration.

If the partnership does not bring peace, it is not alignment; it is distraction. Peace is not the absence of conflict. It is the presence of understanding. Persistent feelings of being unsettled, unheard, or unseen are signals to reevaluate.

When to Say No

Saying no is not rejection. You are allowed to decline partnerships that feel misaligned, unclear, or unsafe.

Whenever a connection pushes you to move faster than wisdom allows, treats the collaboration as a transaction instead of a purposeful exchange, or consistently leaves you feeling drained rather than strengthened, it is a signal that the relationship may not be meant for you.

Partnerships that require you to bend your values, ignore your boundaries, or repeatedly justify your vision ultimately cost more than they contribute. Declining those invitations is not unkind; it is responsible stewardship.

You do not owe anyone access to your vision. You owe your vision protection. A graceful no honors both the person and your purpose. But you must say no when your peace is at stake.

Boundaries are not barriers. They are pathways toward purpose.

Spiritual Discernment in Partnership

Partnership is spiritual. It is not just about compatibility; it is about calling.

Discernment helps you recognize whether someone is truly assigned to this season of your life or whether the connection places your purpose at risk. A spiritually aligned partnership honors God and principles of morality, protects what's been entrusted to you, and brings a sense of steadiness rather than pressure. You can usually feel the difference between a connection rooted in purpose and one rooted in performance.

"For what partnership has righteousness with lawlessness?"
When two people operate from different foundations, values, or intentions, the partnership cannot flow. It will not produce the same fruit.

This is not only about faith. It is about fruit: peace, clarity, growth, and integrity. Not confusion, compromise, or delay.

Spiritual alignment is more than shared belief; it is shared discernment and a mutual sensitivity to divine guidance. This is why careful contemplation should be taken when considering partnerships. Notice what feels steady. Trust the pause.

If you feel rushed, manipulated, or spiritually unsettled, that is not partnership. That is pressure.

Pressure is not the birthplace of purpose.

Emotional Safety in Partnership

Healthy partnership requires emotional safety. You should be able to express concerns without hesitation, engage in conflict without chaos, and show up fully without shrinking yourself. Emotional safety becomes evident in the way disagreements are handled, how respect is demonstrated, and whether your voice is genuinely valued.

When a partnership honors your presence and your perspective, your confidence grows. When it does not, your energy diminishes. Without emotional safety, collaboration becomes performance, and performance leads to burnout.

You are not building for applause; you are building for impact. This is why it matters to choose partners who protect your peace as intentionally as they protect the work. The right partnership strengthens your emotional grounding; the wrong one fractures it.

Strategic Alignment in Partnership

Partnership is not only spiritual and emotional; it is also strategic. Successful collaboration requires shared goals, compatible systems, and mutual accountability. When the workflow, timelines, and communication rhythms align, the work flows with clarity and ease. When they do not, even the strongest emotional bond cannot hold the project together.

Inspiration may create a connection, but strategy sustains it. Effective partnerships pair vision with execution.

For example, a visionary may thrive with someone who brings structure and process. A creative thinker may benefit from someone who understands budgets, contracts, and timelines. A therapist building a practice may need an administrator who values ethics and confidentiality at the same level they value healing.

Strategic alignment ensures that the partnership expands the vision rather than exhausting it. The right collaboration strengthens the work. The wrong one slows it down.

Closing Thought

Partnership is more than joining efforts; it is walking in agreement with someone who honors what you carry.

Choose with intention. Build with wisdom. Protect what has been entrusted to you.

The people you collaborate with become part of your legacy, shaping not only the work you create but the path you walk. Let every partnership reflect clarity, purpose, and peace.

You are allowed to pause, pray, and contemplate. Protect what is precious.

CHAPTER 11

Chapter Eleven

Legacy and Leadership

Pouring Into Others

Often, when we consider the word *legacy*, it is associated with conclusion. In truth, legacy is about continuation.

You've clarified your vision, protected your purpose, built with integrity, and aligned with the right partners. Now comes the question every builder must eventually face:
Once I've built something meaningful, how do I ensure it continues to grow beyond me?

That's legacy.

Legacy is not reserved for parents or public figures. It is not limited to inheritance or institutions. Legacy is influence: intentional, consistent, and deeply personal. It's what you leave behind in the hearts, minds, and spirits of those you've poured into.

Whether you are raising children, mentoring emerging leaders, empowering a team, or nurturing your community, you are shaping legacy every time you offer wisdom, encouragement, or example.

Legacy Is Stewardship

Your purpose was never meant to stop with you. It is meant to flow through you.

Legacy begins when what you build becomes a resource for others. Your gifts are not just tools for personal advancement; they are vessels of insight, healing, and possibility. You are a creator, a cultivator, a leader, and a multiplier.

You do not need a title to influence someone's development. Legacy forms in your presence, in your choices, and in the way you show up for others with intention.

Integrating Purpose and Family

Your family, whether chosen or biological, is part of your legacy. They are witnesses to your process, recipients of your energy, and reflections of your values.

You don't need to sacrifice purpose to be present. You can pursue your vision while nurturing your relationships. Bring your loved ones into the heart behind your work. Let them see your process, not only your results.

Legacy is formed in small moments: a child watching you prepare with excellence, a partner hearing you speak life over your goals, a friend observing you honor your boundaries.

You are modeling purpose every time you choose integrity over urgency, clarity over chaos, and love over ego.

Modeling Purpose to the Next Generation

The next generation watches how you build, not just what you build. They learn from your consistency, your courage, and your character. You do not need perfection; you need presence.

Model purpose by showing up even when it is inconvenient, speaking truth with grace, practicing rest and renewal, and owning your mistakes with humility. Legacy grows through the habits they witness and the posture you carry.

Mentorship as Ministry

Mentorship is an extension of your purpose. It is rooted in presence, care, and responsibility for the growth of another. When you mentor, you offer your story, your scars, and your strategies. You become a mirror for reflection, a map for direction, and a mantle of possibility.

Mentorship becomes ministry or supportive healing when it is led by love, humility, and spiritual awareness. Guidance offered with care creates space for others to grow into their own strength and clarity. Leadership scholars have long emphasized that true leadership is measured by the dignity, development, and growth of people entrusted to one's care (De Pree, 1989).

Impact grows when you walk beside someone as they discover their own voice.

Mentorship is legacy in motion.

Legacy as Continuation, Not Conclusion

Legacy is the ongoing ripple of your obedience, excellence, and consistency. It is what continues to unfold long after you've stepped back, what keeps growing because you invested, and what holds strength because you remained faithful. You don't need to finish everything to leave a legacy. Plant well.

Purpose leaves traces in quiet but powerful ways: in the leader who steps forward with confidence because you once encouraged them, in the child who chooses integrity because you showed what it looks like, in the community that rises because your presence made a difference.

Impact outlasts visibility.

Closing Thought

Your purpose is not meant to stop with you. It is meant to flow through you. Legacy grows through the seeds you plant in others and through the way you show up, speak life, and model purpose in everyday moments. It is not about being remembered. It is about transfer. It is about continuation.

But pouring into others does not require abandoning yourself. Legacy is sustained through balance and guided by boundaries. You lead best when you protect your capacity, honor your limits, and allow yourself to be replenished. Sustainability, not exhaustion, is what keeps your influence steady, strong, and meaningful.

You are already shaping legacy through the way you live, love, and lead. So build boldly. Lead wisely. Pour generously, but never from an empty place. Your influence is purposeful stewardship. Let it flow.

Chapter 12

Chapter Twelve

When Purpose Becomes Primary

The Transition Season

There comes a moment in every builder's journey when you sense a shift. Your nine-to-five, once the centerpiece of your daily rhythm, starts to feel like a supporting chapter. It still sustains you; it still holds purpose, but it no longer defines you. Something greater rises within you, and the work you do outside of your job begins to carry more weight, more clarity, and more of your heart.

This is the essence of Nine to Five On the Side. Your job becomes the side work, and your assignment becomes the main work. You are no longer evaluating your value by a paycheck or a title. You are building a life rather than simply earning a living. You are growing into the truth that your purpose does not fit inside someone else's system forever.

There will be a stage when your nine-to-five or your service within another organization no longer aligns with the expansion of your own vision. The hours you invest in someone else's mission begin to compete with what God has entrusted to you. That recognition is not rebellion. It is revelation. The moment when you understand that transition is approaching.

But transition begins internally long before it becomes external.

Recognizing the Shift

The shift rarely arrives loudly. It emerges as a quiet knowing, a steady pull toward what you are called to create. You begin showing a level of excellence, creativity, and discipline in your own work that matches, or even surpasses, what you once poured into your job. You sense that your gifts require more space. You recognize that your vision needs more time. You feel the weight of a calling that no longer fits into the margins of your schedule.

This chapter is not about abandoning responsibility or rushing out of frustration. It is about discernment, preparation, and timing. It is about acknowledging that your side work has matured, your foundation has strengthened, and your purpose is now ready for more of you.

You are not discarding your job. You are repurposing it. It becomes a place of refinement, observation, and discipline rather than the center of your identity. You learn what you need to learn while knowing that this environment is temporary provision, not permanent definition.

Working With, Not For

As your purpose comes into focus, you begin to see your nine-to-five differently. You stop saying, *"I work for this company,"* and begin understanding that *you work with them.* You bring value. You bring skill. You bring perspective. Your calling is broader than any one office, classroom, clinic, or organization.

Your workplace becomes part of your training ground rather than the center of your identity. You no longer seek validation from systems that were never designed to measure divine progress. Instead, you carry yourself with the awareness that every environment is temporary, but purpose is permanent.

That shift in posture is the beginning of release.

The Moment of Release

Eventually, your purpose will require more of you. It will call for more presence, more creativity, more focus, and more faith. What was once side work will grow too large to stay contained. You will feel the need to redirect time, energy, and attention to the work you were designed to lead.

This release is not a reaction to discomfort. It is a response to readiness. You are not running away from a job. You are walking toward an assignment.

The same excellence you once offered in someone else's system will now be invested in your own. What began as a parallel pursuit becomes the full expression of who you are.

Recognizing the Right Time

The timing of transition is not random. It reveals itself through many signals, often subtle but persistent.

You notice a growing pull toward your purpose that you can no longer dismiss. Your current role begins to feel restrictive instead of supportive. Opportunities within your own vision start accelerating faster than the opportunities at work. You sense that staying for comfort may cost you the fullness of your calling.

These moments are not signs of impatience. They are indicators of growth.

By the time you reach this stage, the work you have done throughout this book becomes your preparation. You have strengthened your discipline, developed your mastery, established credibility, protected your intellectual property, and learned to create systems that sustain you.

Transition then becomes a step from stability into alignment rather than a jump from pressure into panic.

Established Plans

Purpose is not a gamble when it is rooted in divine partnership. Scripture reminds us, "Commit to the Lord whatever you do, and He will establish your plans." This truth is an anchor. You bring your faith, your preparation, and your obedience. God provides timing, clarity, and establishment.

This assurance steadies you when uncertainty rises. You are not walking into an empty space. You are stepping into what has been prepared for you all along.

Closing Thought

There will come a moment when your focus shifts from supporting someone else's vision to fully stewarding your own. You will honor the seasons that shaped you, the lessons that refined you, and the work that strengthened you. But you will also recognize when it is time to step forward.

For most, transition won't be a sudden leap. It will be a steady progression. Purpose does not rush you. It reveals itself gradually. It does not require force. It forms through consistency and willingness and does not demand perfection.

When you embrace purpose as your primary work, you reclaim your time, your energy, and your mission. The creativity, discipline, and devotion that once supported someone else's goals now serve the assignment you were meant to lead.

Transition may feel uncertain, but it is also liberating. You were not created to remain in the margins of your purpose. You were created to lead it.

Your nine-to-five was preparation.
Your purpose is the priority.
It always has been.

Scriptural Appendix & Index

Chapter 1
"Write the vision and make it plain upon tablets, that he may run who reads it." -Habakkuk 2:2

"For it will be like a man going on a journey, who called his servants and entrusted to them his property. To one he gave five talents, to another two, to another one, each according to his ability. Then he went away." -Matthew 25:14–15 (The Parable of Talents paraphrased)

Chapter 2
"We have different gifts, according to the grace given to each of us." -Romans 12:6

Chapter 3
"Be wise as serpents and harmless as doves." -Matthew 10:16

"Do not be conformed to the pattern of this world, but be transformed by the renewing of your mind, that you may prove what is that good and acceptable and perfect will of God." -Romans 12:2

Chapter 4
"There is a time for everything, and a season for everything" -Ecclesiastes 3:1

"A time to be quiet and a time to speak." -Ecclesiastes 3:7

Chapter 5

"Work willingly at whatever you do, as though you were working for the Lord rather than for people." -Colossians 3:23 (NLT)
"To whom much is given, much is required." -Luke 12:48

Chapter 6

"Let perseverance finish its work so that you may be mature and complete, not lacking anything." -James 1:4

Chapter 7

"Bad company corrupts good character." -1 Corinthians 15:33
"Two people are better off than one, for they can help each other succeed." -Ecclesiastes 4:9

Chapter 8

"Good planning and hard work lead to prosperity, but hasty shortcuts lead to poverty." -Proverbs 21:5
"Give to Caesar what is Caesar's, and to God what is God's." -Matthew 22:21

Chapter 9

"For God has not given us a spirit of fear and timidity, but of power, love, and self-discipline." -2 Timothy 1:7

Chapter 10

"Can two people walk together without agreeing on the direction?" -Amos 3:3
"As iron sharpens iron, so a friend sharpens a friend." -Proverbs 27:17

Chapter 11

"The memory of the righteous is a blessing, but the name of the wicked will rot." -Proverbs 10:7

"A good person leaves an inheritance for their children's children." -Proverbs 13:22

Chapter 12

"The plans of the diligent lead surely to abundance, but everyone who is hasty comes only to poverty." -Proverbs 21:5

"Commit to the Lord whatever you do, and He will establish your plans." -Proverbs 16: 3

Bibliography

Alimpić, F., Milovanović, J., Pielech, R., Hinkov, G., Jansson, R., Dufour, S., Beza, M., Bilir, N., Santos del Blanco, L., Božič, G., Bruno, D., Chiarabaglio, P. M., Doncheva, N., Gültekin, Y. S., Ivanković, M., Kelly-Quinn, M., La Porta, N., Nonić, M., Notivol, E., … Rodríguez-González, P. M. (2022). *The status and role of genetic diversity of trees for the conservation and management of riparian ecosystems: A European experts' perspective. Journal of Applied Ecology.*

Brackman, L. (2009). *Jewish wisdom for business success: Lessons from the Torah and other ancient texts.* AMACOM.

Bureau of Economic Analysis. (n.d.). *National economic accounts.* U.S. Department of Commerce. https://www.bea.gov

Bureau of Labor Statistics. (n.d.). *Economic data and labor statistics.* U.S. Department of Labor. https://www.bls.gov

Clear, J. (2018). *Atomic habits: An easy & proven way to build good habits & break bad ones.* Avery.

Csikszentmihalyi, M. (1996). *Creativity: Flow and the psychology of discovery and invention.* HarperCollins.

De Pree, M. (1989). *Leadership is an art.* Doubleday.

Einstein, A. (1945). *Mozart: His character, his work.* Oxford University Press.

Ericsson, A. K., & Pool, R. (2016). *Peak: Secrets from the new science of expertise*. Houghton Mifflin Harcourt.

Federal Reserve System. (n.d.). *Economic research and data*. https://www.federalreserve.gov

Friedman, M. (1962). *Capitalism and freedom*. University of Chicago Press.

Gardner, H. (1983). *Frames of mind: The theory of multiple intelligences*. Basic Books.

Golden, M. (n.d.). *Educational lectures and business training content*. https://myrongolden.com

Internal Revenue Service. (n.d.). *Tax code, forms, and publications*. U.S. Department of the Treasury. https://www.irs.gov

Lapin, D. (2009). *Thou shall prosper: Ten commandments for making money*. Wiley.

Mischel, W. (2014). *The marshmallow test: Mastering self-control*. Little, Brown and Company.

Newport, C. (2016). *Deep work: Rules for focused success in a distracted world*. Grand Central Publishing.

Penrose, R. (1981). *Picasso: His life and work* (3rd ed.). University of California Press.

Renzulli, J. S. (1978). What makes giftedness? A reexamination of a definition. *Gifted Child Quarterly*.

Sadie, S. (1982). *Mozart: The early years*. W. W. Norton & Company.

Smith, A. (2007). *An inquiry into the nature and causes of the wealth of nations*. Harriman House. (Original work published 1776)

The Holy Bible. (n.d.). *King James Version; New International Version; New Living Translation*. Scripture quoted directly by text; verse locations indexed separately.

U.S. Department of the Treasury. (n.d.). *Tax policy and fiscal operations*. https://home.treasury.gov

U.S. Small Business Administration. (n.d.). *Small business guides and resources*. https://www.sba.gov

USA.gov. (n.d.). *Business and self-employment resources*. https://www.usa.gov/business

White Plumbing Co. (n.d.). *Company operations and service model documentation*. https://www.whiteplumbingco.com/